MY PERSONAL GOAL PLANNER

NAME:

YEAR:

DEDICATION

This Goal Planner is dedicated to all the people out there who want to track their Goals and document their findings in the process.

You are my inspiration for producing books and I'm honored to be a part of keeping all of your Goal Planning notes, and records organized.

This journal notebook will help you record your details about tracking your goals for the new year.

Thoughtfully put together with these sections to record: Personal Goals, Productivity Plan, Career Goals, Financial Goals, Travel Goals, Family Goals, Spiritual Goals, Fitness Goals and much, much more!

HOW TO USE THIS BOOK

The purpose of this book is to keep all of your Goal Planning notes all in one place. It will help keep you organized.

This Goal Planner Book will allow you to accurately document every detail about all of the goals in your life. It's a great way to chart your course by setting and meeting your goals.

Here are examples of the prompts for you to fill in and write about your experience in this book:

1. Top 3 Personal Goals For The Year - with actions steps & how you'll stay motivated.
2. Yearly Habits Tracker - with an undated calendar.
3. Quarterly Goals - with take action steps.
4. Weekly Goals - with action plan and notes.
5. Monthly Goals - each month, with action steps you need and notes.
6. Daily Goals - with action steps and notes.
7. Productivity Plan - with space to score yourself 1-10.
8. Goal Action Plan - with notes.
9. Goal Planner - with space to track progress & completion.
10. Mini Goal Planner
11. Goal Tracker - with space to track progress.
12. Monthly Progress
13. Monthly Habit Tracker
14. Success Planner - document action plan and milestones.
15. Career Goals - list goal, action steps and progress.
16. Personal Goals - list goal, action steps and progress.
17. Financial Goals - list goal, action steps and progress.
18. Travel Goals - list goal, action steps and progress.
19. Family Goals - list goal, action steps and progress.
20. Spiritual Goals - list goal, action steps and progress.
21. Fitness Goals - list goal, actions and progress.

QUARTERLY *Goals*

GOALS **ACTION STEPS**

Third Quarter

QUARTERLY Goals

GOALS **ACTION STEPS**

Second quarter

QUARTERLY *Goals*

GOALS **ACTION STEPS**

First

YEARLY HABIT *Tracker*

Start your new year off right by developing positive habits that help you achieve your personal and career goals. Use the charts below to document your progress.

HABIT GOAL

1	2	3	4	5	6	7
8	9	10	11	12	13	14
15	16	17	18	19	20	21
22	23	24	25	26	27	28
29	30	31	MONTH OF:			

HABIT GOAL

1	2	3	4	5	6	7
8	9	10	11	12	13	14
15	16	17	18	19	20	21
22	23	24	25	26	27	28
29	30	31	MONTH OF:			

HABIT GOAL

1	2	3	4	5	6	7
8	9	10	11	12	13	14
15	16	17	18	19	20	21
22	23	24	25	26	27	28
29	30	31	MONTH OF:			

HABIT GOAL

1	2	3	4	5	6	7
8	9	10	11	12	13	14
15	16	17	18	19	20	21
22	23	24	25	26	27	28
29	30	31	MONTH OF:			

HABIT GOAL

1	2	3	4	5	6	7
8	9	10	11	12	13	14
15	16	17	18	19	20	21
22	23	24	25	26	27	28
29	30	31	MONTH OF:			

HABIT GOAL

1	2	3	4	5	6	7
8	9	10	11	12	13	14
15	16	17	18	19	20	21
22	23	24	25	26	27	28
29	30	31	MONTH OF:			

HABIT GOAL

1	2	3	4	5	6	7
8	9	10	11	12	13	14
15	16	17	18	19	20	21
22	23	24	25	26	27	28
29	30	31	MONTH OF:			

HABIT GOAL

1	2	3	4	5	6	7
8	9	10	11	12	13	14
15	16	17	18	19	20	21
22	23	24	25	26	27	28
29	30	31	MONTH OF:			

DATE:

NEW YEAR'S *Goal*

TOP 3 PERSONAL GOALS FOR THIS YEAR

1.
2.
3.

DATE	ACTION STEPS	
		☐
		☐
		☐
		☐
		☐
		☐
		☐
		☐
		☐
		☐
		☐
		☐
		☐
		☐

NOTES

HOW YOU'LL STAY MOTIVATED

NEW YEAR *Wish*

Kick your new year off with a resolution that will bring you happiness. Write down your wish, dreams and goals for the upcoming year.

this will be my year!

QUARTERLY *Goals*

GOALS   ACTION STEPS

Fourth

WEEKLY *Goals*

WEEK OF:

MONDAY

TUESDAY

WEDNESDAY

THURSDAY

FRIDAY

SATURDAY

SUNDAY

TOP GOAL OF THE WEEK

ACTION PLAN

MY NOTES

MONTH:

MONTHLY Goals

GOAL #1　　　　　　**GOAL #2**　　　　　　**GOAL #3**

ACTION STEPS　　　　　　　　　　　NOTES & SCRIBBLES

MONDAY　　TUESDAY　　WEDNESDAY　　THURSDAY　　FRIDAY　　SATURDAY　　SUNDAY

TODAY'S Goal

DATE:

TOP GOALS OF THE DAY
1
2
3
4
5

NOTES

TIME STARTED	TIME FINISHED	ACTION STEPS
:	:	
:	:	
:	:	
:	:	
:	:	
:	:	
:	:	
:	:	
:	:	
:	:	
:	:	
:	:	
:	:	
:	:	

3 Week PRODUCTIVITY Plan

Keep track of the days you are productive and score yourself from 1-10.

PRODUCTIVITY LEVELS (1-UNPRODUCTIVE, 10 VERY PRODUCTIVE)

REFLECT ON YOUR OVERALL PRODUCTIVITY

WEEK One

M	01	02	03	04	05	06	07	08	09	10
T	01	02	03	04	05	06	07	08	09	10
W	01	02	03	04	05	06	07	08	09	10
T	01	02	03	04	05	06	07	08	09	10
F	01	02	03	04	05	06	07	08	09	10
S	01	02	03	04	05	06	07	08	09	10
S	01	02	03	04	05	06	07	08	09	10

WEEK Two

M	01	02	03	04	05	06	07	08	09	10
T	01	02	03	04	05	06	07	08	09	10
W	01	02	03	04	05	06	07	08	09	10
T	01	02	03	04	05	06	07	08	09	10
F	01	02	03	04	05	06	07	08	09	10
S	01	02	03	04	05	06	07	08	09	10
S	01	02	03	04	05	06	07	08	09	10

WEEK Three

NOTES

M	01	02	03	04	05	06	07	08	09	10
T	01	02	03	04	05	06	07	08	09	10
W	01	02	03	04	05	06	07	08	09	10
T	01	02	03	04	05	06	07	08	09	10
F	01	02	03	04	05	06	07	08	09	10
S	01	02	03	04	05	06	07	08	09	10
S	01	02	03	04	05	06	07	08	09	10

DATE:

Goal ACTION PLAN

NOTES:

Goal PLANNER

DATE

GOAL:

START DATE:

GOAL OVERVIEW:

ACTION STEPS

PROGRESS

COMPLETED

Mini Goal PLANNER

GOAL:

START DATE:

OVERVIEW

ACTION STEPS

PROGRESS

GOAL:

START DATE:

OVERVIEW

ACTION STEPS

PROGRESS

Goal TRACKER

GOAL	PROGRESS	✓

Monthly PROGRESS

JANUARY	FEBRUARY	MARCH

APRIL	MAY	JUNE

JULY	AUGUST	SEPTEMBER

OCTOBER	NOVEMBER	DECEMBER

HABIT *Tracker*

Forming productive habits that improve your life and help you reach your goals is important. Choose a personal or business goal and work towards developing a habit that supports it.

HABIT #1:

START DATE:

END DATE:

M O T I V A T I O N

1	2	3	4	5	6	7
8	9	10	11	12	13	14
15	16	17	18	19	20	21
22	23	24	25	26	27	28
29	30	31				

HABIT #2:

START DATE:

END DATE:

M O T I V A T I O N

1	2	3	4	5	6	7
8	9	10	11	12	13	14
15	16	17	18	19	20	21
22	23	24	25	26	27	28
29	30	31				

HABIT #3:

START DATE:

END DATE:

M O T I V A T I O N

1	2	3	4	5	6	7
8	9	10	11	12	13	14
15	16	17	18	19	20	21
22	23	24	25	26	27	28
29	30	31				

SUCCESS *Planner*

USE THE SPACE BELOW TO DOCUMENT YOUR MILESTONES & ACTION PLAN

NOTES & DOODLES

GOALS
stay focused & motivated

USE THE FOLLOWING PAGES TO IDENTIFY YOUR CAREER, PERSONAL, FINANCIAL, TRAVEL, FAMILY, FITNESS & SPIRITUAL GOALS.

JANUARY Goals

SUNDAY	MONDAY	TUESDAY	WEDNESDAY	THURSDAY	FRIDAY	SATURDAY

JANUARY NOTES

_____
_____
_____
_____
_____
_____
_____

FEBRUARY Goals

SUNDAY	MONDAY	TUESDAY	WEDNESDAY	THURSDAY	FRIDAY	SATURDAY

FEBRUARY Goals

FEBRUARY NOTES

_____
_____
_____
_____
_____
_____
_____

MARCH Goals

SUNDAY	MONDAY	TUESDAY	WEDNESDAY	THURSDAY	FRIDAY	SATURDAY

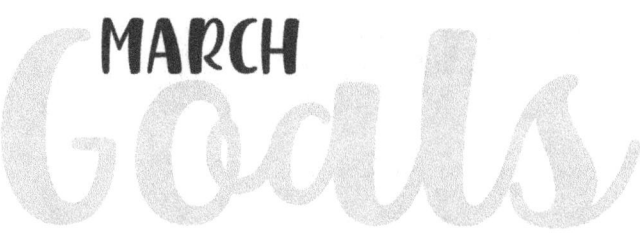

MARCH NOTES

_____
_____
_____
_____
_____
_____
_____

APRIL Goals

SUNDAY	MONDAY	TUESDAY	WEDNESDAY	THURSDAY	FRIDAY	SATURDAY

APRIL NOTES

MAY Goals

SUNDAY	MONDAY	TUESDAY	WEDNESDAY	THURSDAY	FRIDAY	SATURDAY

MAY NOTES

_____
_____
_____
_____
_____
_____
_____

JUNE Goals

SUNDAY	MONDAY	TUESDAY	WEDNESDAY	THURSDAY	FRIDAY	SATURDAY

JUNE Goals

JUNE NOTES

_____
_____
_____
_____
_____
_____

JULY Goals

SUNDAY	MONDAY	TUESDAY	WEDNESDAY	THURSDAY	FRIDAY	SATURDAY

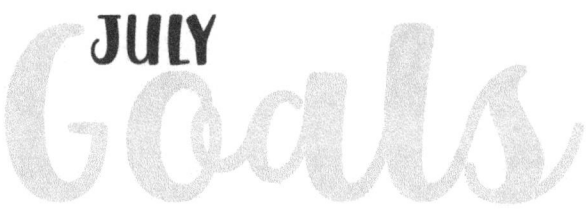

JULY NOTES

AUGUST Goals

SUNDAY	MONDAY	TUESDAY	WEDNESDAY	THURSDAY	FRIDAY	SATURDAY

AUGUST Goals

AUGUST NOTES

_____
_____
_____
_____
_____
_____
_____

SEPTEMBER *Goals*

SUNDAY	MONDAY	TUESDAY	WEDNESDAY	THURSDAY	FRIDAY	SATURDAY

SEPTEMBER Goals

SEPTEMBER NOTES

_____
_____
_____
_____
_____
_____
_____

OCTOBER Goals

SUNDAY	MONDAY	TUESDAY	WEDNESDAY	THURSDAY	FRIDAY	SATURDAY

OCTOBER Goals

OCTOBER NOTES

_____
_____
_____
_____
_____
_____
_____

NOVEMBER Goals

SUNDAY	MONDAY	TUESDAY	WEDNESDAY	THURSDAY	FRIDAY	SATURDAY

NOVEMBER Goals

NOVEMBER NOTES

_____
_____
_____
_____
_____
_____
_____

DECEMBER Goals

SUNDAY	MONDAY	TUESDAY	WEDNESDAY	THURSDAY	FRIDAY	SATURDAY

DECEMBER NOTES

_____
_____
_____
_____
_____
_____
_____

YEAR

this will be my year!

FINANCIAL Goals

DOCUMENT YOUR FINANCIAL GOALS & ACCOMPLISHMENTS

TOP FINANCIAL GOAL ☆	SECONDARY GOAL ☆

GOAL	ACTION STEPS
	PROGRESS:

GOAL	ACTION STEPS
	PROGRESS:

GOAL	ACTION STEPS
	PROGRESS:

GOAL	ACTION STEPS
	PROGRESS:

GOAL	ACTION STEPS
	PROGRESS:

TRAVEL *Goals*

DOCUMENT YOUR TRAVEL GOALS & ACCOMPLISHMENTS

TOP TRAVEL GOAL ☆	SECONDARY GOAL ☆

GOAL	ACTION STEPS
	PROGRESS:

GOAL	ACTION STEPS
	PROGRESS:

GOAL	ACTION STEPS
	PROGRESS:

GOAL	ACTION STEPS
	PROGRESS:

GOAL	ACTION STEPS
	PROGRESS:

FAMILY Goals

DOCUMENT YOUR FAMILY GOALS & ACCOMPLISHMENTS

TOP FAMILY GOAL ☆	SECONDARY GOAL ☆

GOAL	ACTION STEPS
	PROGRESS:

GOAL	ACTION STEPS
	PROGRESS:

GOAL	ACTION STEPS
	PROGRESS:

GOAL	ACTION STEPS
	PROGRESS:

GOAL	ACTION STEPS
	PROGRESS:

SPIRITUAL *Goals*

DOCUMENT YOUR SPIRITUAL GOALS & ACCOMPLISHMENTS

TOP SPIRITUAL GOAL ☆	SECONDARY GOAL ☆

GOAL	ACTION STEPS
	PROGRESS:

GOAL	ACTION STEPS
	PROGRESS:

GOAL	ACTION STEPS
	PROGRESS:

GOAL	ACTION STEPS
	PROGRESS:

GOAL	ACTION STEPS
	PROGRESS:

FITNESS Goals

DOCUMENT YOUR FITNESS GOALS & ACCOMPLISHMENTS

TOP FITNESS GOAL	SECONDARY GOAL

GOAL	ACTION STEPS
	PROGRESS:

GOAL	ACTION STEPS
	PROGRESS:

GOAL	ACTION STEPS
	PROGRESS:

GOAL	ACTION STEPS
	PROGRESS:

GOAL	ACTION STEPS
	PROGRESS:

GOALS
stay focused & motivated

ACTION Plan

Monday

Tuesday

Wednesday

Thursday

Friday

Saturday

Sunday

NEW YEAR Wins

Document your milestones and accomplishments throughout the year.

2 RECENT WINS

TOP 3 MILESTONES

1.
2.
3.

3 THINGS I'VE LEARNED ABOUT MYSELF OVER THE LAST YEAR

PERSONAL REFLECTIONS | HOW I'VE LEARNED TO COPE WITH EMOTIONS

PERSONAL REFLECTIONS	HOW I'VE LEARNED TO COPE WITH EMOTIONS

NOTES

www.ingramcontent.com/pod-product-compliance
Lightning Source LLC
Chambersburg PA
CBHW081237080526
44587CB00022B/3971